ed emberley's
CRAZY
MIXED-UP
face game

73851

SLUGGO

LIBRARY OF CONGRESS CATALOGING IN PUBLICATION DATA

EMBERLEY, ED.
   ED EMBERLEY'S CRAZY MIXED-UP FACE GAME.

   1. CREATIVE ACTIVITIES AND SEAT WORK -- JUVENILE
LITERATURE.   2. GAMES -- JUVENILE LITERATURE.
I.TITLE.   II.TITLE: CRAZY MIXED-UP FACE GAME.
GV1203.E44   794   80-25361
ISBN 0-316-23420-6
ISBN 0-316-23421-4 (PBK.)

FIRST EDITION
PUBLISHED SIMULTANEOUSLY IN CANADA BY LITTLE, BROWN AND COMPANY (CANADA) LIMITED
PRINTED IN THE UNITED STATES OF AMERICA

YOU CAN USE ANY OTHER METHOD OF NUMBER
SELECTING AS LONG AS IT HAS NUMBERS FROM 1 TO 12
PLUS A WAY TO WIN A "FREE CHOICE".

FREE CHOICE

1.

12.

JOKER

FREE CHOICE

12. 11.

J A

1.

★	1	2	★
3	4	5	6
7	8	9	10
★	11	12	★

NO DICE --(YOU
CANNOT ROLL A
ONE WITH DICE)

THINGS YOU WILL NEED TO PLAY THIS GAME:

1. THIS BOOK   2. A PENCIL   3. SCISSORS

4. PAPER FOLDED LIKE THIS →

FOLD   FOLD   UNFOLD

5. A NUMBER SELECTOR

HOW TO MAKE AN "OFFICIAL FACE GAME NUMBER SELECTOR."

FOLD   FOLD   UNFOLD   FOLD   FOLD   UNFOLD   NUMBER   CUT   CUT

YOU CAN PLACE SLIPS FACE DOWN TO PLAY.

IF NUMBERS SHOW THROUGH...

...YOU CAN PUT THEM IN A BOX OR OTHER CONTAINER TO PLAY.

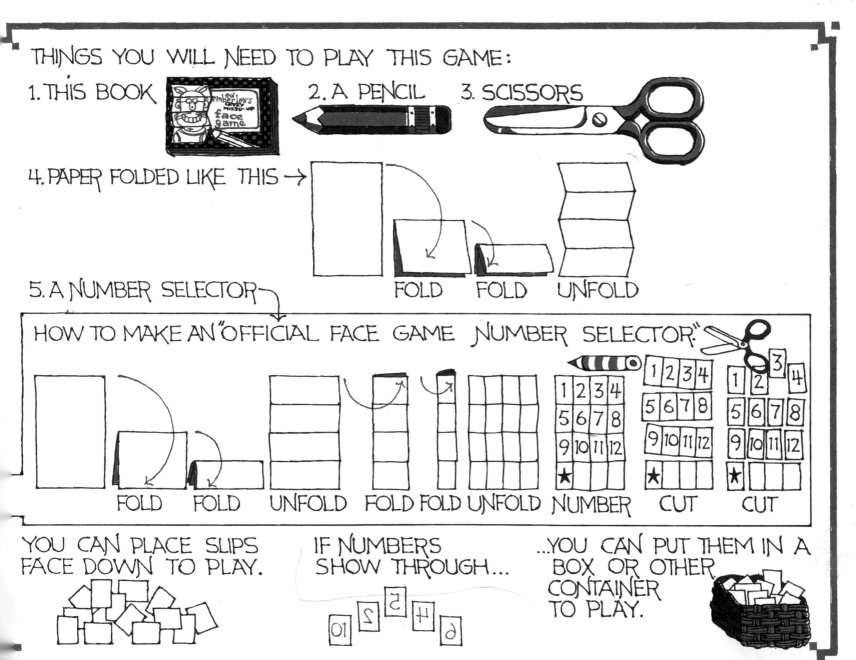

how to play

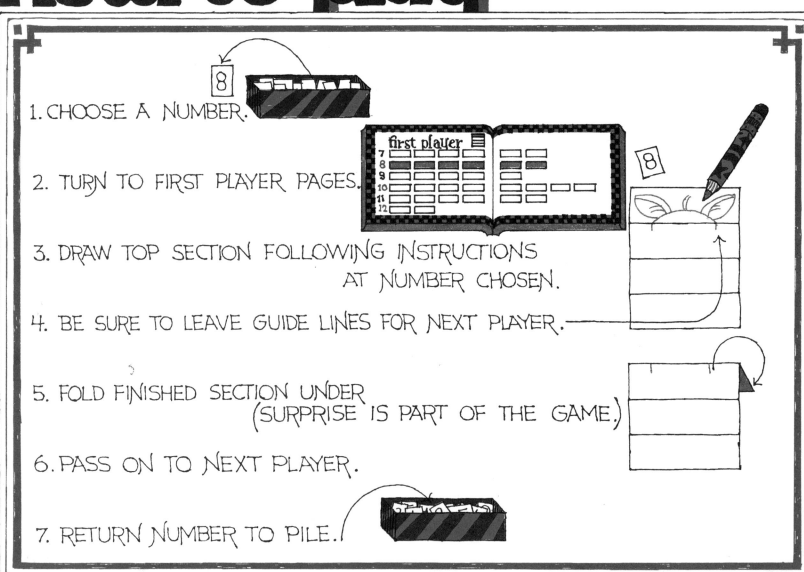

1. CHOOSE A NUMBER.

2. TURN TO FIRST PLAYER PAGES.

3. DRAW TOP SECTION FOLLOWING INSTRUCTIONS AT NUMBER CHOSEN.

4. BE SURE TO LEAVE GUIDE LINES FOR NEXT PLAYER.

5. FOLD FINISHED SECTION UNDER (SURPRISE IS PART OF THE GAME.)

6. PASS ON TO NEXT PLAYER.

7. RETURN NUMBER TO PILE.

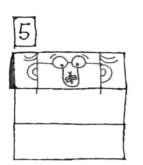
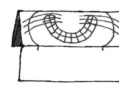

8 PLAY CONTINUES UNTIL
   ALL FOUR PARTS OF
   FACE ARE FINISHED.

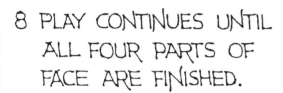

9. UNFOLD PAPER TO
   SEE WHAT KIND OF
   CRAZY, MIXED UP FACE
   YOU HAVE CREATED!

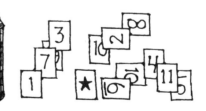

★ IF YOU CHOOSE A STAR, YOU MAY:
   CHOOSE ANY NUMBER YOU WANT...
   OR, CHOOSE A PART FROM THE "FREE CHOICE" PAGE...
   OR, MAKE UP A PART OF YOUR OWN.

1 LUDWIG

2 LONELL

3 LINDER

4 LESTER

5 LEONARD

6 LUCRETIA

7 LARS

8 LIMPA

 LULU

10 LYLE

11 LORENZO

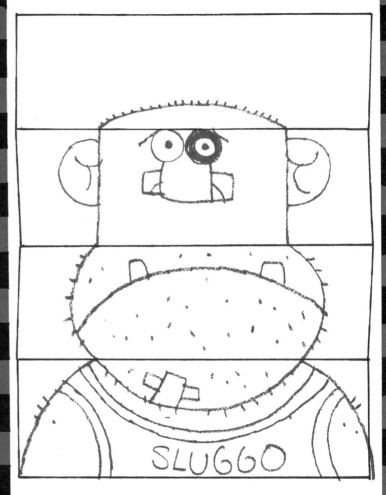

SLUGGO

12 LLEWELLYN

first player

1
2
3
4
5
6

LOOK UNDER HERE TO SEE WHAT TO DRAW

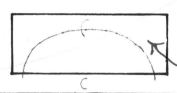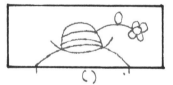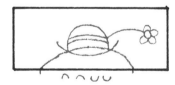

LOOK UP HERE TO SEE WHERE TO PUT IT

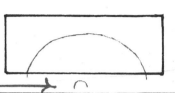

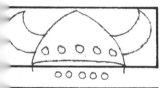

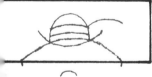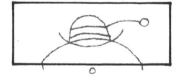

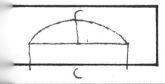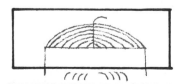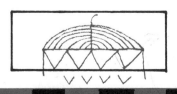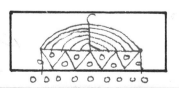

first player

7

8

9

10

11

12

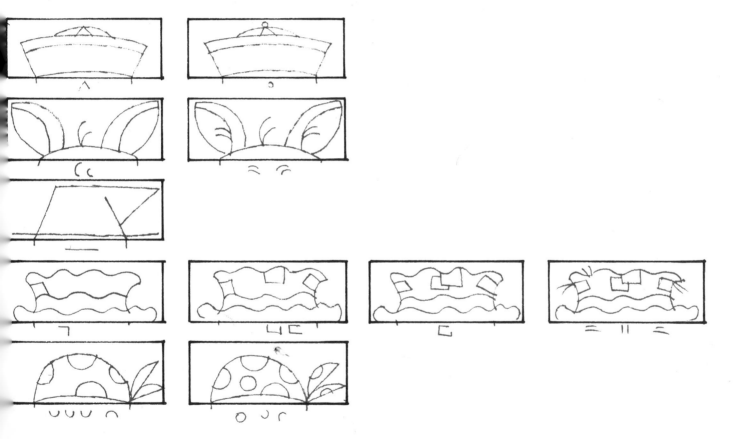

second player

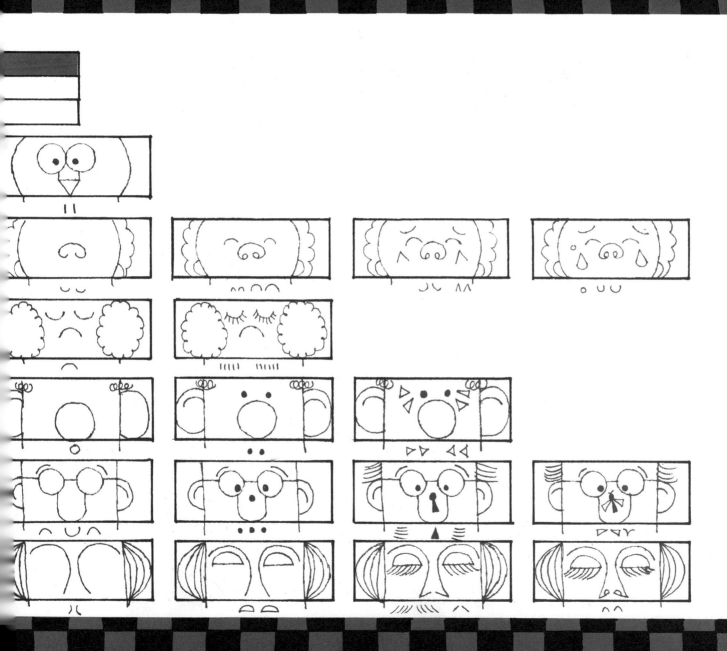

second player

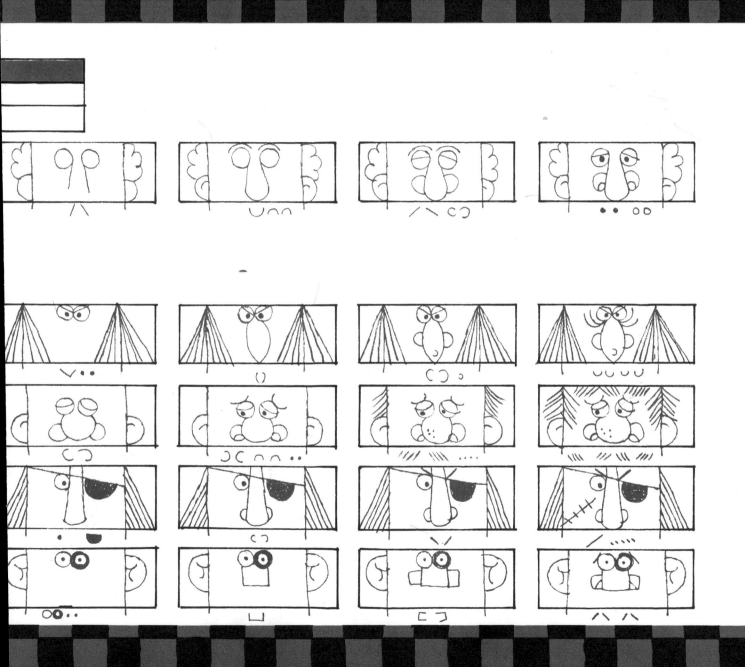

third player

1
2
3
4
5
6

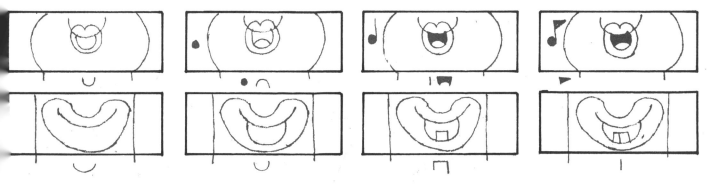

 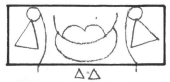 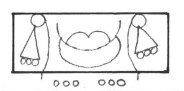

third player

7
8
9
10
11
12

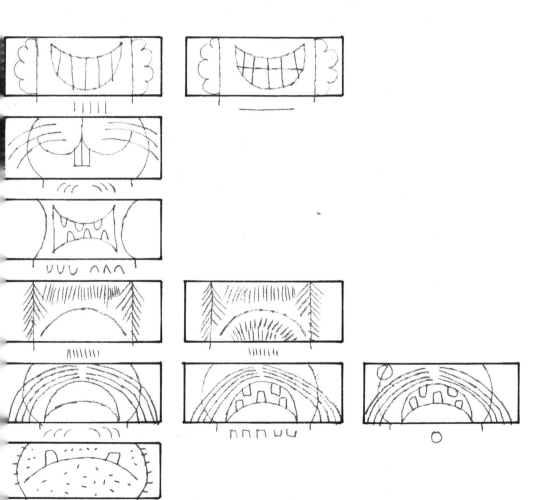

fourth player

1
2
3
4
5
6

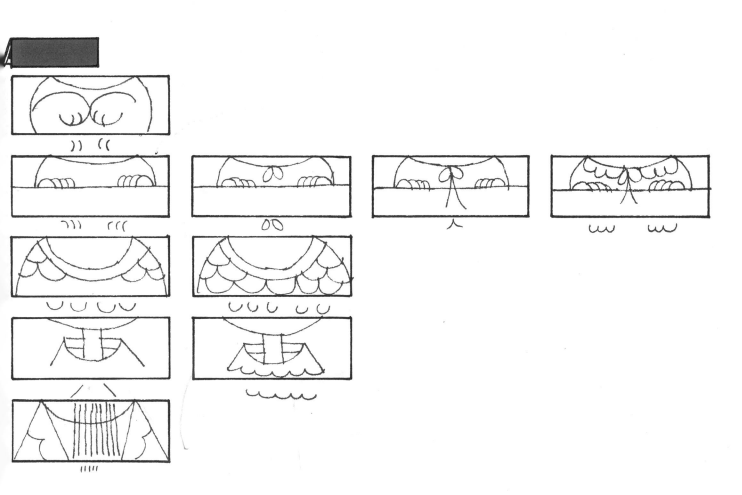

fourth player

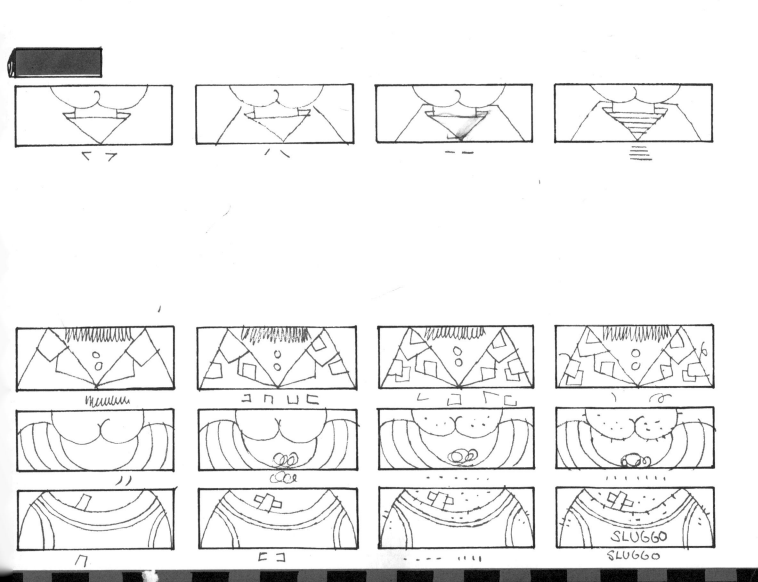

SLUGGO

SLUGGO

free choice